BEGINNER GUIDE

AI AGENTS IN EVERYDAY LIFE

How AI Agents Are Transforming Daily Tasks

AI Personal Assistants: The Future of Productivity

=

TABLE OF CONTENTS

Chapter 8: Health and Wellness

- Health Data Monitoring and Analysis
- Medication Management and Reminders
- Fitness Planning and Progress Tracking
- Mental Health Support and Cognitive Behavioral Interventions
- Telemedicine and Healthcare Navigation
- Case Study: Managing Chronic Conditions with AI Support

PART III: TECHNOLOGY BEHIND THE SCENES

Chapter 9: Large Language Models and Foundation Models

- The Architecture of Modern LLMs
- Training Methodologies and Data Requirements
- Fine-Tuning and Specialization Techniques
- Inference Optimization and Deployment Strategies
- The Evolution from Models to Multimodal Systems
- Limitations and Challenges in LLM Development

Chapter 10: Reasoning and Decision-Making Capabilities

- From Pattern Matching to Reasoning
- Chain-of-Thought and Tree-of-Thought Approaches
- Planning and Sequential Decision Making
- Tool Use and External System Integration
- Multi-Agent Systems and Collaborative Problem Solving
- Current Limitations in AI Reasoning

Chapter 11: AI Agent Deployment Technologies

Foreword

The pace at which artificial intelligence has transformed from a specialized research field into an integral part of our daily lives is nothing short of remarkable. Just a decade ago, voice assistants were novel technologies with limited capabilities; today, AI agents serve as personal assistants, creative collaborators, and problem-solving partners across virtually every domain of human activity.

As we stand at this technological inflection point, it becomes increasingly important to understand not just what AI agents can do, but how they're fundamentally reshaping our relationship with technology and productivity. This book arrives at a crucial moment when millions of people are incorporating AI assistants into their workflows, homes, and daily routines—yet many lack a comprehensive understanding of these tools' capabilities, limitations, and future trajectory.

The author has created an essential guide for navigating this new landscape, offering both practical insights for immediate application and deeper technological context for those seeking to understand the systems that increasingly mediate our digital experiences. Whether you're a technology professional looking to optimize your workflow, an educator preparing students for an AI-augmented future, or simply someone interested in making the most of these powerful new tools, this book provides valuable perspectives on how AI agents are transforming productivity and daily life.

What makes this work particularly valuable is its balance between accessibility and technical depth. Rather than treating AI as magical or inscrutable, it illuminates the underlying systems and design principles that enable today's AI agents while remaining grounded in practical, real-world applications.

As we continue to navigate the integration of increasingly capable AI into our lives and work, resources like this book become essential tools for ensuring we harness these technologies thoughtfully and effectively.

Introduction

The Rise of AI Agents in the Modern World

In early 2023, an inflection point occurred in our relationship with artificial intelligence. While voice assistants and recommendation algorithms had been part of our digital landscape for years, the emergence of sophisticated large language models and generative AI systems marked a fundamental shift. Almost overnight, millions of people gained access to AI assistants capable of writing essays, generating images, answering complex questions, and engaging in nuanced conversations.

This technological leap forward didn't merely introduce new tools—it created the foundation for a new paradigm in how humans interact with computers. We've entered the age of AI agents: software entities designed to perceive their environment, make decisions, and take actions to achieve specific goals on behalf of their users. These systems combine multiple AI capabilities—language understanding, reasoning, specialized knowledge, and environmental awareness—into unified interfaces that can adapt to our needs and preferences over time.

The implications of this shift are profound. Tasks that once required significant human time and attention can now be delegated to AI agents that operate with increasing autonomy and capability. From scheduling meetings to researching complex topics, from managing household systems to optimizing financial decisions, AI agents are transforming productivity across personal and professional domains.

This transformation isn't happening in isolation. It's occurring alongside other technological trends that amplify its impact: the proliferation of smart devices, the expansion of sensor technologies, improvements in speech recognition and synthesis, and the development of sophisticated API ecosystems. Together, these advances are creating an environment where AI agents can become increasingly integrated into the fabric of everyday life.

From Science Fiction to Reality: The Evolution of AI Personal Assistants

For decades, science fiction has painted visions of intelligent computer assistants that understand natural language, anticipate needs, and seamlessly manage both digital and physical environments. From HAL 9000 in "2001: A Space Odyssey" to JARVIS in the Iron Man films, these fictional AI systems represented an aspirational future where technology could understand and respond to human intentions rather than requiring humans to adapt to technological limitations.

The path from these fictional depictions to today's AI assistants has been neither straight nor simple. Early attempts at natural language interfaces, like the ELIZA program from the 1960s, relied on simple pattern matching rather than genuine understanding. The first commercial voice assistants introduced in the early 2010s could respond to specific commands but struggled with conversational context, complex queries, or tasks requiring reasoning.

What changed in the early 2020s was the convergence of three critical factors:

1. Massive improvements in language models: The development of transformer-based neural networks and their scaling to hundreds of billions of parameters enabled

systems with unprecedented language understanding and generation capabilities.

2. Multimodal integration: AI systems gained the ability to process and generate multiple types of data—text, images, audio, and structured information—creating more versatile and capable assistants.

3. Tool and API integration: AI assistants evolved from closed systems to platforms that could connect with external services, databases, and computational tools, dramatically expanding their capabilities.

This technological evolution has brought us to a point where AI personal assistants are not just convenient voice-activated tools but increasingly sophisticated agents capable of complex task completion, creative collaboration, and personalized support across diverse contexts.

How This Book Will Help You Navigate the AI Revolution

This book serves as both a practical guide and a technological overview of the AI agent revolution. Whether you're looking to optimize your productivity with existing AI tools, understand the capabilities and limitations of current systems, or prepare for future developments, you'll find valuable insights in the chapters ahead.

We'll begin by establishing a foundational understanding of AI agents—what they are, how they work, and the technological developments that have enabled their current capabilities. This section will demystify concepts like large language models, reasoning systems, and multimodal AI, providing a clear picture of the technologies behind today's assistants.

The core of the book explores how AI agents are transforming specific domains of everyday life—from home management to professional productivity, from education to financial planning. Each chapter in this section not only describes current applications but also examines real-world use cases and offers practical guidance for integrating AI assistants into your own workflows and routines.

We'll then take a deeper dive into the technological infrastructure that powers these systems, examining the architecture of modern AI agents, the challenges in their development and deployment, and the emerging capabilities that will shape their future evolution.

Finally, we'll consider the broader implications of increasingly autonomous and capable AI assistants—exploring ethical considerations, potential societal impacts, and what the future might hold as these technologies continue to advance.

By the end of this book, you'll have gained not only practical knowledge about leveraging today's AI agents but also a deeper understanding of how these systems work and where they're headed. Whether you're an early adopter looking to maximize the value of cutting-edge tools or someone seeking to understand a technological shift that's rapidly transforming our relationship with computers, you'll find value in the exploration ahead.

Let's begin our journey into the world of AI agents and discover how they're reshaping productivity, creativity, and everyday life in the 21st century.

PART I: UNDERSTANDING AI AGENTS

Chapter 1: What Are AI Agents?

Defining AI Agents and Their Core Components

At their most fundamental level, AI agents are software systems designed to perceive their environment, make decisions based on those perceptions, and take actions to achieve specific goals—all with varying degrees of autonomy. Unlike traditional software that follows rigid, predefined paths, AI agents can adapt their behavior based on their observations, learn from experience, and operate in environments with uncertainty.

The concept of an agent implies several key characteristics:

- Goal-oriented behavior: AI agents work toward accomplishing specific objectives, whether those are explicit tasks assigned by users or implicit goals derived from understanding user needs.

- Environmental perception: Agents must sense or observe the world around them, whether that's through processing text inputs, analyzing images, receiving data from sensors, or monitoring digital systems.

Action execution: Agents influence their environment by taking actions, which might include generating text responses, controlling smart home devices, making API calls to external services, or creating digital content.

A complete AI agent system typically comprises several interconnected components:

1. Perception module: Interprets inputs from users or sensors, converting raw data into structured representations that the agent can reason about.

2. Knowledge base: Stores information about the world, including both general knowledge and personalized data about user preferences and history.

3. Reasoning engine: Processes perceptions and knowledge to determine appropriate actions, often using a combination of neural networks, symbolic reasoning, and specialized algorithms.

4. Action module: Executes decisions by generating outputs, controlling connected systems, or interfacing with external services.

5. Learning component: Enables the agent to improve its performance over time based on feedback and experience.

The sophistication of each component and how they integrate determines an agent's overall capabilities and limitations.

The Distinction Between AI Agents and Traditional Software

While the boundary between AI agents and conventional software is increasingly blurred, several key distinctions help clarify what makes an agent approach unique:

Adaptability vs. Fixed Behavior

Traditional software follows predetermined logic paths coded explicitly by developers. Given the same inputs under the same conditions, it will always produce identical outputs. AI agents, by contrast, can adapt their behavior based on experience, feedback, and changing contexts. They may respond differently to similar situations as they learn what approaches are most effective.

Autonomy vs. Direct Control

Conventional applications require explicit instructions for each action they take. AI agents operate with varying degrees of autonomy—they might independently determine how to accomplish goals, decide which information is relevant, or even prioritize between competing objectives. This shift from "tool" to "assistant" represents a fundamental change in how we interact with technology.

Goal-Oriented vs. Function-Oriented

Traditional software is typically organized around specific functions or features that users must combine to achieve their goals. AI agents are increasingly organized around goals themselves—users express what they want to accomplish, and the agent determines how to achieve it, potentially coordinating multiple systems and services behind the scenes.

Natural vs. Structured Interfaces

Conventional applications rely on structured interfaces (buttons, forms, menus) that users must learn to navigate. AI agents increasingly support natural language interfaces where users express their needs conversationally, without needing to understand the underlying system organization.

Contextual Understanding vs. Stateless Operation

Many traditional software systems are relatively stateless, treating each interaction independently. AI agents maintain contextual awareness across interactions, remembering previous exchanges, user preferences, and ongoing tasks to provide more coherent and personalized experiences.

Types of AI Agents: From Reactive to Self-Learning

AI agents exist along a spectrum of complexity and capability:

1. Simple Reflex Agents

These basic agents operate using condition-action rules, selecting actions based solely on current perceptions without considering history or context. A simple chatbot that matches user inputs to predefined responses falls into this category. While limited, these agents can be effective for narrow, well-defined tasks with clear input patterns.

2. Model-Based Reflex Agents

These agents maintain an internal model of the world that tracks aspects of the environment that aren't directly observable in the current perception. A smart thermostat that remembers temperature patterns over time exemplifies this approach—it doesn't just react to current temperature but considers historical patterns to make better decisions.

3. Goal-Based Agents

Goal-based agents evaluate potential actions based on how they contribute to achieving specified objectives. They consider the future consequences of actions rather than just immediate responses. Virtual assistants that develop multi-step plans to accomplish user tasks (like "plan my vacation") operate as goal-based agents.

4. Utility-Based Agents

These agents extend goal-based reasoning by evaluating actions according to how well they maximize a utility function—essentially a measure of "goodness" that can balance multiple competing objectives. Recommendation systems that optimize for both user satisfaction and diversity of suggestions exemplify this approach.

5. Learning Agents

Learning agents improve their performance over time through experience. They modify their behaviors based on feedback, adapting to user preferences and changing environments. Modern AI assistants that personalize their responses based on user interactions represent this category.

6. Autonomous Agents

The most sophisticated agents combine all the above capabilities with advanced reasoning and self-modification abilities. They can operate independently for extended periods, manage complex goals, and even adjust their own objective functions based on higher-level principles. Fully autonomous personal assistants that proactively manage multiple aspects of a user's digital life represent an emerging example of this category.

As of 2025, most commercial AI assistants combine elements from several of these categories, with significant advances in learning capabilities and goal-based reasoning, though fully autonomous operation remains an active area of development.

The Agent-Environment Interface: How AI Perceives and Acts

The relationship between an AI agent and its environment—whether that's a digital ecosystem, a physical space monitored through sensors, or the conceptual space of a conversation—is defined by what the agent can perceive and what actions it can take.

Perception Channels

Modern AI agents perceive their environment input channels:

- Text input: The primary interface for many AI assistants, allowing them to process questions, commands, and information from users.
- Voice and audio: Speech recognition enables voice-based interaction, while audio processing can detect environmental sounds, music, or other acoustic signals.

- Visual perception: Computer vision capabilities allow agents to process images, videos, documents, and visual environments.
- Structured data: Agents often have access to databases, APIs, and structured information sources that provide organized data about specific domains.
- Sensor data: For agents integrated with smart home systems or IoT devices, environmental sensors provide information about physical conditions like temperature, motion, or air quality.

The richness and accuracy of these perception channels significantly influence an agent's ability to understand context and make appropriate decisions.

Action Capabilities

AI agents influence their environment through various output channels:

- Text generation: Producing written responses, summaries, creative content, or structured documents.

- Voice synthesis: Converting text responses into natural-sounding speech.

- Visual content creation: Generating or editing images, diagrams, or videos.

- Digital system control: Interacting with other software systems through APIs, database queries, or direct integration.

- Physical system control: For agents connected to smart home systems or robotics, issuing commands that affect the physical environment.

- Information storage: Maintaining memories, user preferences, or contextual information for future interactions.

The breadth of these action capabilities determines what tasks an agent can perform independently versus where it must rely on human intervention.

Feedback Loops

The agent-environment interface isn't just about immediate perceptions and actions—it also encompasses feedback mechanisms that allow agents to learn and improve:

- Explicit feedback: Direct ratings, corrections, or instructions from users that indicate successful or unsuccessful interactions.

- Implicit feedback: Behavioral signals like whether users follow an agent's recommendations or continue engaging with its outputs.

- Environmental feedback: Changes in the environment that result from the agent's actions, providing information about their effectiveness.

Key Technological Foundations: Machine Learning, Natural Language Processing, and Computer Vision

Modern AI agents build upon several core technological foundations that have seen dramatic advances in recent years:

Machine Learning and Neural Networks

The ability to learn from data rather than following explicitly programmed rules underpins most modern AI agents. Key developments include:

- Deep learning: Neural networks with multiple layers that can automatically extract features and patterns from raw data, enabling more sophisticated perceptual capabilities.

- Reinforcement learning: Techniques that allow agents to learn optimal behaviors through trial and error, maximizing rewards and minimizing penalties.

- Transfer learning: Methods for applying knowledge gained in one domain to new but related problems, dramatically improving efficiency and reducing data requirements.

- Few-shot and zero-shot learning: Capabilities that allow models to perform tasks with minimal or no specific examples, leveraging patterns learned from broader training.

Natural Language Processing

NLP capabilities form the backbone of how most AI assistants interact with users:

- Transformer architectures: Neural network designs that revolutionized language processing by capturing long-range dependencies and contextual relationships in text.

- Large language models (LLMs): Massive neural networks trained on diverse text corpora that can understand and generate human language with unprecedented fluency and contextual awareness.

- Semantic understanding: The ability to grasp meaning beyond keywords, including nuance, implication, and contextual references.

- Conversational context management: Techniques for maintaining coherent discussions across multiple turns, remembering previous statements \

Computer Vision

Visual perception capabilities extend what AI agents can understand and process:

- Object recognition: Identifying and categorizing objects within images or video streams.

- Scene understanding: Comprehending spatial relationships, activities, and contextual elements in visual media.

- Document processing: Extracting structured information from forms, receipts, diagrams, and other visual documents.

- Multimodal integration: Combining visual and textual information to develop more comprehensive understanding.

- Knowledge Representation and Reasoning

How agents organize and use information affects their decision-making capabilities:

- Knowledge graphs: Structured representations of entities and their relationships that support reasoning about complex domains.

- Symbolic reasoning: Logic-based approaches that complement neural methods for tasks requiring

- Causal reasoning: Understanding cause-effect relationships rather than just statistical correlations.

- Planning algorithms: Techniques for developing multi-step action sequences to achieve goals.

Together, these technological foundations provide the capabilities that enable AI agents to understand complex instructions, reason about user goals, and take appropriate actions across diverse contexts. While each foundation has its own limitations and challenges, their integration into unified agent architectures has created systems with capabilities that would have seemed impossible just a few years ago.

Chapter 2: The Evolution of AI Personal Assistants

Historical Context: From ELIZA to Modern AI Assistants

The journey toward today's AI personal assistants spans over six decades, marked by fundamental breakthroughs, technological limitations, and shifting paradigms in how we conceptualize human-computer interaction.

Early Conversational Systems (1960s-1970s)

The concept of communicating with computers through natural language has captivated researchers since the earliest days of computing. ELIZA, developed by Joseph Weizenbaum at MIT in 1966, represented one of the first attempts to create the illusion of conversation with a machine. Using simple pattern matching and substitution techniques, ELIZA could imitate a Rogerian psychotherapist by reflecting user statements back as questions, creating a surprisingly engaging experience despite having no actual understanding of the conversation.

SHRDLU, created by Terry Winograd in 1970, demonstrated more sophisticated natural language understanding within a limited domain—a virtual world of blocks that the program could manipulate based on textual commands. While restricted to a tiny universe,

SHRDLU showed how language understanding could connect to action and environmental perception.

These early systems were significant not for their capabilities, which were extremely limited by today's standards, but for establishing the vision of natural language as an interface paradigm and highlighting the immense challenges involved in true language understanding.

Expert Systems and Knowledge-Based Approaches (1980s-1990s)

The 1980s saw a shift toward expert systems—programs designed to emulate human expertise in specialized domains through extensive knowledge bases and rule systems. Systems like MYCIN (medical diagnosis) and DENDRAL (chemical analysis) demonstrated impressive capabilities within narrow domains but required enormous effort to program and couldn't adapt beyond their predefined knowledge.

By the 1990s, personal digital assistants (PDAs) like Apple's Newton introduced the concept of mobile assistants, though their functionality was limited to basic organization tools with rudimentary natural language capabilities. These early consumer products highlighted both the appeal and limitations of assistant-like technology in everyday contexts.

Web-Based and Early Mobile Assistants (2000s)

The early 2000s brought Ask Jeeves (later Ask.com) and similar services that framed web search as a conversational experience, encouraging users to pose natural language questions rather than keyword combinations. While innovative in interface design, these systems ultimately relied on traditional search algorithms rather than true language understanding.

SmarterChild, a popular chatbot available on messaging platforms like AIM and MSN Messenger, provided a glimpse of how conversational interfaces might integrate with everyday digital activities, offering weather updates, movie times, and other information through a text-based interface.

The First Wave of Voice Assistants (2011-2019)

The modern era of AI assistants began with the introduction of Siri by Apple in 2011, followed by Google Now (2012), Microsoft Cortana (2014), and Amazon Alexa (2014). These systems represented a significant leap forward, combining:

- Speech recognition technology for voice input
- Natural language processing for command interpretation
- Cloud-based processing for greater capability than device-only solutions
- Integration with smartphone functions and third-party services

- Personality elements designed to create more engaging interactions

However, these first-generation assistants had significant limitations:

- Limited contextual understanding, treating each query as largely independent
- Narrow capabilities focused on specific commands and queries
- Minimal reasoning capabilities beyond simple if-then logic
- Frequent misunderstandings and inability to handle complex requests

Despite these constraints, voice assistants gained widespread adoption, with smart speakers bringing them into millions of homes and establishing voice control as a mainstream interaction method.

The Foundation Model Revolution (2019-2025)

The landscape of AI assistants underwent a dramatic transformation beginning around 2019, driven by the development of increasingly powerful language models based on transformer architectures. This evolution proceeded through several key phases:

1. Early Large Language Models (2019-2020): GPT-2 and similar models demonstrated unprecedented text generation capabilities, though with limited reliability and factual grounding.

2. Multimodal Integration (2021-2022): Systems began combining language understanding with image recognition, speech processing, and other modalities, creating more versatile assistants.

3. Reasoning-Augmented Models (2023-2024): Techniques like chain-of-thought prompting, tool use, and external knowledge integration dramatically improved assistants' ability to solve complex problems and perform multi-step tasks.

4. Agent Architectures (2024-2025): The most recent evolution has moved toward agent-based frameworks where assistants can maintain goals over time, use tools autonomously, and adapt their behavior based on user feedback and environmental context.
   This rapid progression has transformed AI assistants from simple command-response systems to collaborative partners capable of complex task completion, creative contribution, and increasingly autonomous operation.

Technological Breakthroughs That Enabled Today's AI Agents

Several key technological breakthroughs enabled the transition from rudimentary assistants to the sophisticated AI agents available today:

Transformer Neural Network Architecture

Introduced in the 2017 paper "Attention Is All You Need," the transformer architecture revolutionized natural language processing by enabling models to process text in parallel (rather than sequentially) while maintaining awareness of relationships between words regardless of their distance in the text. This breakthrough:

- Dramatically improved the quality of language understanding and generation
- Enabled more efficient training on massive text datasets
- Created a scalable architecture where larger models consistently showed improved capabilities
- Formed the foundation for all major language models powering today's AI assistants

Large-Scale Pre-Training

The approach of pre-training models on vast corpora of text before fine-tuning them for specific applications proved transformative. This methodology:

- Allowed models to develop broad language understanding and world knowledge
- Created foundation models that could be adapted to numerous downstream tasks
- Reduced the amount of task-specific training data needed for new applications
- Enabled zero-shot and few-shot learning where models could perform tasks with minimal explicit examples

Reinforcement Learning from Human Feedback (RLHF)

Traditional supervised learning proved insufficient for training assistants that needed to be helpful, harmless, and honest. RLHF emerged as a crucial approach where:

- Human evaluators rate model outputs based on quality and alignment with human preferences
- These ratings train a reward model that can evaluate new outputs
- Reinforcement learning optimizes the assistant to maximize this reward function
- The process creates models that better align with human expectations and values

Multimodal Integration

The ability to process and generate multiple types of content—text, images, audio, structured data—dramatically expanded assistant capabilities:

- Vision-language models enabled understanding of images alongside text
- Multimodal learning allowed knowledge transfer between different forms of information
- Unified architectures could handle diverse input types through consistent internal representations
- Generated outputs could combine multiple modalities for richer communication

Tool Use and External System Integration

Perhaps the most significant recent advancement has been enabling language models to use external tools and systems:

- Function calling capabilities allow models to determine when to use specialized tools
- API integration connects language intelligence to external data sources and services
- Code interpretation enables computation and data manipulation beyond what's possible in pure language generation
- Retrieval augmentation provides access to specific information not captured in model parameters

Reasoning Enhancement Techniques

Specialized techniques have dramatically improved the reasoning capabilities of AI systems:

- Chain-of-thought prompting encourages step-by-step reasoning rather than jumping to conclusions
- Tree-of-thought approaches explore multiple reasoning paths to find optimal solutions
- Self-critique methods allow models to evaluate and revise their own outputs
- Planning modules help break complex tasks into manageable steps

Together, these technological breakthroughs have transformed AI assistants from limited voice command systems to versatile agents capable of understanding complex contexts, reasoning through difficult problems, and taking actions across multiple domains and modalities.

The Shift from Command-Based to Conversational Interfaces

One of the most fundamental transformations in AI assistant evolution has been the shift from command-based to truly conversational interfaces. This transition represents not just a technical advancement but a reimagining of how humans and computers interact.

Command-Based Paradigm (2011-2019)

Early voice assistants operated primarily through command detection. Users needed to:

- Use specific trigger phrases or wake words ("Hey Siri," "Alexa")
- Issue requests in predictable formats that matched predefined patterns
- Frame questions or instructions using particular syntax the system could recognize
- Learn which command structures worked for different types of requests
- Remember the specific capabilities the assistant supported

This approach put the burden of adaptation on the human user, who needed to learn how to communicate in ways the system could understand. Interactions were predominantly transactional—a user would issue a command, the assistant would execute it or respond, and the interaction would end.

Early Conversational Attempts (2019-2021)

As natural language processing improved, assistants began incorporating more conversational elements:

- Limited context awareness allowed follow-up questions without restating the topic
- Assistants could handle some variation in phrasing and command structure
- Simple clarification requests could resolve ambiguity in user instructions
- Personality features created more engaging response patterns
- Turn-taking became more natural with improved latency and interruption handling

However, these systems still struggled with truly open-ended conversations, complex contextual references, and understanding implicit user needs that weren't explicitly stated.

Genuinely Conversational Interfaces (2022-2025)

The latest generation of AI assistants operates with fundamentally different interaction paradigms:

- Natural language understanding: Users can express needs in their own words, without conforming to specific command structures or learning specialized vocabulary.

- Contextual awareness: Assistants maintain conversation history and understanding across multiple turns, remembering references, resolving pronouns, and building on previously established information.

- Intent recognition: Rather than matching commands to predefined functions, systems identify underlying user goals and determine how to address them, even when expressed indirectly.

- Mixed-initiative interaction: Conversations can be driven by either the user or the assistant, with the assistant proactively offering relevant information, suggesting related capabilities, or requesting clarification when needed.

- Repair mechanisms: When misunderstandings occur, assistants can gracefully recover through clarification questions, offering alternatives, or adjusting their understanding based on feedback.

- Adaptive communication style: Systems adjust their language, level of detail, and formality based on user preferences and contextual appropriateness.

This shift has profound implications for usability, accessibility, and the types of tasks assistants can support:

- Reduced cognitive load: Users no longer need to remember specific commands or learn system-specific interaction patterns.

- Accessibility improvements: People with varying technical expertise, language proficiency, or cognitive abilities can interact more successfully with conversational systems.

- Support for complex tasks: Multi-step processes that would be cumbersome to execute through discrete commands become manageable in a conversational format where context builds naturally.

- Relationship building: Truly conversational interfaces create a sense of ongoing relationship rather than isolated transactions, potentially increasing user comfort and trust.

While challenges remain—including handling very long-term context, truly understanding implicit meaning, and managing conversational repairs gracefully—the trajectory is clear: AI assistants are increasingly adapting to human communication patterns rather than requiring humans to adapt to technological limitations.

Major Milestones in AI Assistant Development (2011-2025)

2011: Apple Introduces Siri – The First Mainstream AI Assistant

- Apple Siri became the first widely adopted AI-powered virtual assistant, integrated into iPhones.
- Based on voice recognition and rule-based NLP, Siri could handle simple tasks like setting reminders, sending texts, and answering basic questions.
- Despite its limited contextual understanding, Siri marked the beginning of AI assistants as a consumer product.

2014: Amazon Alexa and the Smart Speaker Revolution

- Amazon launched Alexa, transforming AI assistants from mobile-exclusive tools into home-based smart devices.
- The Amazon Echo smart speaker pioneered always-on voice interaction, allowing hands-free commands for controlling smart home devices.
- Alexa's "Skills" ecosystem introduced third-party integrations, enabling developers to create custom functionalities.
- This milestone accelerated the adoption of AI assistants in everyday home automation.

2016: Google Assistant Brings Context-Aware AI to Smartphones

- Google introduced Google Assistant, featuring improved conversational AI and context awareness compared to Siri and Alexa.
- Unlike previous AI assistants, Google Assistant could remember context across multiple queries, enabling natural, multi-turn conversations.
- It integrated seamlessly with Google services, allowing users to manage emails, calendars, and smart home devices via voice commands.
- The assistant's integration with Android devices increased its global accessibility and adoption.

2018: AI Assistants Achieve Human-Like Conversations (Google Duplex)

- Google Duplex demonstrated AI-powered phone call automation, allowing AI to book appointments and make reservations with human-like speech.
- The system introduced realistic voice synthesis, natural pauses, and contextual adaptation, making AI sound more human.
- This milestone showcased the potential of AI assistants in customer service and real-world applications.

2019: AI Assistants Become Multimodal with Vision and Text Capabilities

- AI assistants evolved beyond voice-based interactions, incorporating text, images, and multimodal inputs.
- Google Assistant and Alexa gained visual interfaces on smart displays, allowing users to interact using touchscreens and images.
- BERT (Bidirectional Encoder Representations from Transformers), a breakthrough in NLP, improved AI assistants' ability to understand the meaning of words in context, enhancing response accuracy.

2020–2021: GPT-3 and AI Assistants with Advanced Natural Language Understanding

- GPT-3 (OpenAI) marked a revolution in AI-generated text, enabling AI assistants to generate human-like responses across a vast range of topics.
- AI assistants like ChatGPT, Jasper AI, and Copy.ai leveraged GPT-3 for creative content generation, chatbot automation, and conversational AI.
- AI customer service chatbots became more responsive and capable of handling complex queries with minimal human intervention.

2022: AI Assistants Gain Reasoning and Tool-Use Capabilities

- AI assistants moved beyond simple Q&A interactions, incorporating Chain-of-Thought (CoT) reasoning, enabling them to explain reasoning steps in complex problem-solving.
- AI-powered tools integrated real-time information retrieval, allowing assistants to provide live stock prices, weather updates, and factual responses beyond their training data.
- API integration allowed AI assistants to connect with productivity tools like Google Docs, Notion, and Slack, increasing workplace automation.

2023: ChatGPT and the AI Boom – A New Era of AI Assistants

- OpenAI launched ChatGPT, a conversational AI assistant capable of engaging in natural, multi-turn discussions with contextual memory.
- ChatGPT reached 100 million users in two months, making it one of the fastest-growing AI applications in history.
- Microsoft integrated ChatGPT into Bing AI Search, transforming search engines into AI-powered conversational assistants.

- AI-powered copilots emerged in software development (GitHub Copilot), writing (Notion AI), and customer support (Intercom AI).
- AI assistants became customizable with the introduction of fine-tuning and prompt engineering techniques.

2024: AI Assistants Become Multimodal and Interactive (GPT-4 & Gemini AI)

- AI assistants evolved into multimodal AI systems, processing and generating text, images, videos, and audio.
- GPT-4, Gemini AI, and Claude AI enhanced AI assistants with:
  - Real-time speech-to-text and text-to-image generation (e.g., DALL·E 3).
  - Memory and context retention, enabling personalized, long-term interactions.
  - Task automation, where AI could write code, summarize documents, and analyze spreadsheets autonomously.
- Voice-based AI avatars enabled human-like digital assistants for virtual meetings and customer interactions.

2025: AI Assistants Move Towards Autonomous Agents and Personal AI Companions

- AI assistants transition from passive responders to proactive autonomous agents, capable of taking actions independently.
- Auto-GPT and AgentGPT demonstrate AI agents that:

  - Plan and execute tasks automatically without step-by-step human prompts.
  - Interact with external apps, APIs, and databases to perform complex workflows.
  - Manage long-term projects, such as scheduling meetings, drafting reports, and optimizing business operations.
- AI assistants become personalized digital companions, adapting to individual preferences and emotions.
- The rise of voice-enabled humanoid robots integrates AI assistants into robotics for home, healthcare, and industrial automation.

Chapter 3 Core Components: Perception, Reasoning, Learning, and Action

Modern AI agents are designed with four essential components: Perception, Reasoning, Learning, and Action. These elements enable AI to interpret data, make decisions, adapt, and interact effectively with users and their environment.

Perception

AI agents collect and interpret data through various sensory inputs:

- Natural Language Processing (NLP): Helps AI understand and generate human-like text.
- Computer Vision: Allows AI to analyze images and videos.
- Speech Recognition: Converts spoken words into text for processing.
- Sensor Integration: Enables AI to interact with IoT devices and physical environments.

Reasoning

AI applies logical frameworks to make decisions:

- Rule-Based Systems: Operate using predefined logic rules.

- Probabilistic Reasoning: Uses statistical models to predict outcomes.
- Symbolic AI: Employs structured data and logical relationships to infer conclusions.

Learning

AI continuously improves through data-driven learning methods:

- Supervised Learning: Trained on labeled data.
- Unsupervised Learning: Identifies patterns in unlabeled data.
- Reinforcement Learning: Learns via trial and error with rewards.
- Few-shot and Zero-shot Learning: Performs tasks with minimal training data.

Action

AI agents execute decisions through:

- Conversational AI: Engaging users via chatbots and virtual assistants.
- Decision-Making Systems: Providing recommendations and predictions.
- Autonomous Control: Managing robotics and self-driving technologies.

Large Language Models as the Foundation

Modern AI agents rely on Large Language Models (LLMs) like GPT-4 and Gemini. These models enhance AI functionality in various ways:

Key Capabilities of LLMs

- Context Awareness: Retains information over long conversations.
- Personalization: Adapts responses based on user interactions.
- Multi-Turn Conversations: Maintains logical discussion flow.
- Domain-Specific Knowledge: Excels in specialized fields like healthcare, law, and finance.

Applications of LLMs in AI Agents

- Text Generation: Produces human-like content and reports.
- Semantic Search: Extracts relevant insights from vast data sources.
- Code Assistance: Helps with programming and debugging.

Multi-Modal Capabilities: Beyond Text to Vision, Sound, and More

AI is advancing beyond text-based models to multi-modal AI, capable of processing and generating diverse data types.

Key Multi-Modal Features

- Text-to-Image: AI-generated visuals from descriptions (e.g., DALL·E, MidJourney).
- Speech-to-Text & Text-to-Speech: Enables voice-based interaction.
- Image Recognition: AI-powered object and face detection.
- Audio Analysis: Identifies sound patterns in music and speech.

Use Cases

- Creative Content: AI-generated artwork, videos, and music.
- Accessibility Tools: Assisting visually/hearing-impaired users.
- Enhanced HCI (Human-Computer Interaction): Making AI communication more intuitive.

Memory Systems: How AI Agents Maintain Context

AI agents require memory to recall user interactions and deliver intelligent responses.

Types of Memory in AI

- Short-Term Memory: Stores recent conversations.
- Long-Term Memory: Retains data for ongoing user interactions.

- Semantic Memory: Holds structured knowledge about facts and concepts.
- Episodic Memory: Remembers unique user experiences and events.

Benefits of AI Memory Systems

- Continuity: Enables seamless interactions over time.
- Personalization: Customizes responses based on past exchanges.
- Improved Learning: Enhances AI efficiency by leveraging past insights.

Integration Frameworks: APIs, Plugins, and Interoperability Standards

AI agents connect with external systems through APIs, plugins, and interoperability standards to expand their capabilities.

APIs & Plugins

- Chatbot APIs: Integrate AI chat features into applications.
- Automation Plugins: Enable AI-driven task automation.
- Data Access APIs: Retrieve real-time insights from cloud platforms.

Interoperability Standards

- OpenAI Function Calling: Standardized AI interactions.
- ONNX (Open Neural Network Exchange): Cross-platform model compatibility.
- Federated Learning: Enables decentralized AI training for privacy-preserving models.

Future Trends in AI Integration

- Unified AI Ecosystems: Merging various AI tools into one platform.
- Cross-Model Communication: Enabling AI agents to interact across different systems.
- Real-Time Adaptive AI: AI agents responding dynamically to user needs.

Conclusion

The architecture of modern AI agents is a dynamic and evolving field, built on core principles of perception, reasoning, learning, and action. By integrating LLMs, multi-modal capabilities, memory systems, and advanced integration frameworks, AI agents are becoming more intelligent, versatile, and capable of transforming industries. As AI continues to advance, these architectural foundations will shape the next generation of intelligent automation.

Chapter 4: Home Life Transformation

Introduction

AI agents are revolutionizing how we interact with our homes, transforming them into intelligent, automated ecosystems. From smart home management to personalized meal planning and family scheduling, AI-driven systems are enhancing efficiency, security, and convenience.

This chapter explores the real-world applications of AI in home life, highlighting how AI assistants automate tasks, enhance decision-making, and improve quality of life. We will also examine a case study of a fully automated smart home in 2025, providing a glimpse into the near future.

---

1. Smart Home Management and Automation

1.1 AI-Driven Home Automation

AI-powered smart home systems integrate with IoT (Internet of Things) devices to automate household tasks, offering:

- Voice-activated control: AI assistants (Alexa, Google Assistant) manage lights, temperature, and appliances.
- Routine automation: AI learns user habits, automating morning routines (e.g., opening blinds, brewing coffee).
- Remote monitoring: Homeowners can check security cameras, lock doors, and adjust settings via AI apps.

1.2 AI-Enhanced Energy Efficiency

AI optimizes energy usage by analyzing patterns and reducing waste:

- Smart thermostats (Nest, Ecobee) adjust temperature based on occupancy and weather forecasts.
- AI-powered lighting systems turn off unused lights and adjust brightness.
- Solar energy management AI predicts energy consumption and optimizes power storage.

1.3 AI-Driven Home Security

Security systems now integrate AI for real-time threat detection:

- Facial recognition entry ensures only authorized users access the home.
- AI motion sensors differentiate between pets, people, and intruders.

- Predictive analytics detect unusual activity and alert homeowners instantly.

---

2. Meal Planning, Recipe Suggestions, and Dietary Management

2.1 AI-Powered Personalized Meal Planning

AI nutrition assistants analyze dietary preferences, health goals, and allergies to recommend meal plans:

- AI-based meal planners (Yummly, Samsung Food) suggest recipes based on available ingredients.
- Real-time calorie tracking helps users meet fitness goals.
- AI cooking assistants (Chef Watson, SideChef) provide step-by-step cooking guidance.

2.2 Smart Kitchen Integration

AI seamlessly integrates with smart appliances for automated cooking:

- AI-powered ovens (Brava, June Oven) adjust temperatures and cooking times.
- Smart refrigerators (Samsung Family Hub, LG InstaView) track expiration dates and suggest recipes.
- AI beverage machines brew coffee and mix drinks based on user preferences.

2.3 AI for Grocery Shopping and Waste Reduction

AI optimizes grocery shopping and minimizes food waste:

- Automated grocery lists based on AI inventory tracking.
- Price comparison AI finds the best deals online and in-store.
- Food waste reduction AI suggests meals based on expiring ingredients.

---

3. Entertainment Curation and Personalization

3.1 AI-Powered Home Entertainment

AI enhances home entertainment by offering personalized content:

- Streaming AI (Netflix, Spotify, YouTube AI) suggests tailored content based on preferences.
- AI-powered home theaters adjust lighting, sound, and screen settings for an optimal experience.
- Voice-controlled entertainment enables hands-free navigation of content.

3.2 Virtual and Augmented Reality Experiences

AI integrates with VR/AR entertainment systems, offering:

- AI-curated VR gaming experiences based on skill level.
- Immersive AI-powered AR home workouts.
- Personalized AI DJ and AI art curation for music and visual experiences.

3.3 AI in Home Music and Audiobook Selection

- AI-driven smart speakers generate playlists based on mood and activity.
- AI audiobook narrators adjust reading speed and tone based on listener preferences.
- AI-powered karaoke assistants analyze voice pitch and offer real-time feedback.

---

4. Family Scheduling and Coordination

4.1 AI-Assisted Family Calendar Management

AI helps organize family schedules, reminders, and daily plans:

- AI-integrated calendars (Google Calendar AI, Microsoft Outlook AI) schedule events and avoid conflicts.
- AI voice assistants provide real-time reminders for school, work, and social events.
- Smart home hubs synchronize all family members' schedules.

4.2 AI for Childcare and Parenting Support

- AI baby monitors detect unusual baby movements or crying patterns.
- AI tutors (Khanmigo, Squirrel AI) assist children with homework and personalized learning.
- Parental control AI filters content and manages screen time.

4.3 AI-Powered Household Chores Coordination

- Task automation AI (Alexa, Google Home, Apple HomeKit) assigns chores based on schedules.
- Smart robotic cleaners (Roomba, Roborock) use AI to optimize home cleaning.
- AI laundry assistants recommend washing settings based on fabric type.

---

5. Health Monitoring and Wellness Support

5.1 AI-Driven Health Monitoring at Home

AI-powered devices help track and improve family health:

- Wearable AI health monitors (Fitbit, Apple Watch) track heart rate, sleep, and activity.
- Smart home health stations conduct daily health check-ups.

- AI-powered medication reminders ensure timely doses.

5.2 AI for Mental Health and Well-being

- AI chatbots (Wysa, Woebot) provide mental health support.
- Smart lighting AI adjusts brightness to improve sleep and mood.
- AI meditation apps (Calm, Headspace AI) offer guided relaxation sessions.

5.3 AI in Home Fitness and Personal Training

- AI personal trainers (Peloton AI, Tempo AI) create personalized workout routines.
- Smart mirrors (Mirror by Lululemon) provide AI-guided fitness coaching.
- Real-time posture correction AI enhances exercise safety.

Case Study: The Fully Automated Smart Home of 2025

Background

In 2025, The Davis Family upgraded their home with AI-driven smart technology, fully integrating AI automation for efficiency, security, and comfort.

Key Features of Their AI Home:Outcome:

Feature	AI-Driven System	Impact
AI Smart Hub	Unified AI assistant (Google Assistant + Alexa + HomeKit)	Controls all smart devices seamlessly
Energy Optimization	Smart thermostats, AI solar panel management	Reduces energy costs by 35%
Automated Kitchen	AI recipe assistant + smart oven +	Saves 10 hours/week on meal planning

	fridge inventory tracking	
Personalized Entertainment	AI-curated music, VR home theater	Enhances relaxation and leisure
Family Scheduling AI	AI calendar integration with work, school, and social events	Reduces missed appointments by 50%
AI Security System	Facial recognition + smart locks + AI monitoring	Provides real-time security alerts
Health & Wellness AI	Wearable health monitoring + fitness AI + mental health chatbots	Improves family well-being

- AI automation reduced daily manual tasks by 60%.
- AI-powered energy efficiency saved them $1,500 annually.

- The family experienced improved health, productivity, and security.

Conclusion

AI agents are fundamentally reshaping home life, bringing unparalleled convenience, security, and personalization. From smart home automation to AI-powered wellness, homes are becoming autonomous, self-optimizing environments.

As AI technology advances, we move closer to a future where homes predict and fulfill our needs effortlessly, creating a seamless, intelligent living experience.

Chapter 5: Professional Productivity Revolution

In today's fast-paced professional landscape, productivity is no longer just about working harder—it's about working smarter. The integration of artificial intelligence (AI) into workplace operations is revolutionizing the way professionals manage their tasks, optimize workflows, and communicate efficiently. AI-driven tools are enabling individuals to automate mundane activities, focus on high-value work, and make data-driven decisions with greater precision.

This chapter explores how AI is enhancing professional productivity across various domains, including meeting management, research synthesis, document processing, communication, time management, and workflow automation. By understanding these advancements, professionals can harness AI's potential to maximize efficiency and effectiveness.

Meeting Management and Administrative Support

Meetings are a vital part of professional life, yet they often consume valuable time and resources. AI-powered meeting assistants such as Notion AI, Zoom AI Companion, and Otter.ai are transforming the way meetings are scheduled, conducted, and documented.

AI-Enhanced Meeting Features:

- Automated Scheduling: AI scans participants' calendars and finds the best available times.
- Real-Time Transcription: AI captures spoken words and converts them into text.
- Meeting Summarization: AI extracts key points and generates follow-up actions.
- Virtual Meeting Assistants: AI reminds participants of previous discussions and upcoming deadlines.

For instance, a project manager no longer needs to manually coordinate meeting times. An AI assistant automatically schedules the meeting, sends invitations, and even provides a summary of key takeaways afterward. This level of automation saves time and ensures efficiency.

Research and Information Synthesis

Professionals across industries rely on accurate and timely research to make informed decisions. AI-powered tools streamline this process by gathering, analyzing, and summarizing large volumes of information in seconds.

Benefits of AI in Research:

- Automated Data Extraction: AI pulls insights from various sources instantly.
- Content Summarization: AI condenses lengthy reports and articles into digestible information.
- Trend Analysis: AI identifies industry patterns and forecasts future trends.

- Reference Management: AI organizes sources and generates citations.

A content strategist, for example, can use AI to analyze competitor blogs and extract trending topics. This eliminates hours of manual research while ensuring content relevance.

Document Creation, Editing, and Management

Creating, editing, and managing documents is a fundamental aspect of professional life. AI tools enhance this process by improving accuracy, readability, and organization.

AI-Powered Document Solutions:

- Content Generation: AI drafts reports, proposals, and emails.
- Grammar & Style Correction: AI tools like Grammarly refine writing for clarity and professionalism.
- Document Categorization: AI organizes and tags documents based on content.
- Collaboration & Version Control: AI tracks document edits and facilitates seamless teamwork.

For example, a legal professional can leverage AI to draft contracts, proofread documents, and ensure compliance with industry standards—all within minutes.

Email and Communication Assistance

Emails are essential for workplace communication, yet they can be overwhelming. AI-powered assistants help manage email overload, prioritize responses, and automate replies.

AI-Powered Email Capabilities:

- Smart Email Sorting: AI categorizes emails based on priority and content.
- Automated Responses: AI suggests relevant replies to common inquiries.
- Email Summarization: AI extracts key points from long email threads.
- Follow-Up Reminders: AI ensures that important emails receive timely responses.

A sales executive, for instance, can use AI to draft personalized follow-up emails for potential clients, significantly improving engagement rates and response times.

Time Management and Priority Setting

AI-driven productivity tools empower professionals to allocate their time effectively by analyzing work patterns and optimizing schedules.

Time Optimization with AI:

- Task Prioritization: AI highlights high-impact tasks for maximum efficiency.
- Work Pattern Analysis: AI tracks productivity trends and suggests improvements.
- Automated Scheduling: AI integrates with calendars for seamless task management.
- Distraction Control: AI helps minimize interruptions and maintain focus.

For example, an executive receives a daily AI-generated report that outlines priority tasks and suggests the best times for deep-focus work, leading to increased productivity.

Complex Task Automation and Workflow Optimization

Beyond individual productivity, AI streamlines entire business operations by automating repetitive tasks and optimizing workflows.

AI-Driven Automation in Business:

- Data Entry & Processing: AI extracts, organizes, and processes data automatically.
- Inventory & Logistics: AI optimizes supply chain and inventory management.
- Marketing Automation: AI personalizes content distribution and campaign scheduling.

- AI-Powered Customer Support: AI chatbots handle inquiries and improve customer engagement.

An HR manager, for instance, automates the employee onboarding process with AI-driven workflows, reducing paperwork and manual follow-ups while ensuring a smooth experience for new hires.

Case Study: A Day in the Life of an AI-Empowered Professional

To illustrate the impact of AI on professional productivity, let's examine the daily routine of Alex, a Digital Marketing Manager, who seamlessly integrates AI into his workflow.

6:30 AM – AI-generated morning briefing provides industry news and priority tasks.

8:00 AM – Smart email sorting categorizes incoming emails and prioritizes urgent messages.

10:00 AM – AI schedules and summarizes a team meeting, highlighting key takeaways.

1:00 PM – Automated content research provides keyword insights for blog creation.

3:00 PM – Marketing automation tools schedule personalized social media posts.

6:00 PM – AI productivity analysis offers insights on time spent and suggests improvements for the next day.

By leveraging AI, Alex reduces manual workload, enhances decision-making, and focuses on strategic growth initiatives.

Conclusion

The integration of AI in professional settings is revolutionizing productivity. By automating routine tasks, improving communication, and optimizing workflows, AI empowers professionals to work smarter and achieve more in less time.

Chapter 6: Learning and Education

Artificial Intelligence (AI) has revolutionized the education sector, enhancing traditional teaching methods and making learning more personalized, accessible, and efficient. With advancements in machine learning, natural language processing, and data analytics, AI-powered tools now support learners of all ages in diverse educational settings. This chapter explores the role of AI in education, focusing on personalized learning companions, research assistants, creative writing support, language translation, continuous skill development, and case studies of AI tutors in K-12 and higher education.

Personalized Learning Companions

AI-driven personalized learning systems cater to individual student needs, adjusting the pace, difficulty, and style of content delivery based on real-time progress and performance. These AI tutors analyze students' learning patterns and provide customized recommendations, ensuring a more engaging and effective learning experience.

- Adaptive Learning Platforms: Platforms like Coursera, Udemy, and Khan Academy use AI algorithms to suggest tailored courses and resources.

- AI Chatbots for Education: Virtual tutors like Duolingo's chatbot or Socratic by Google assist students by answering queries, explaining concepts, and providing real-time feedback.
- Gamified Learning: AI-enhanced gamification techniques encourage engagement and motivation through rewards, quizzes, and interactive challenges.

Research and Knowledge Synthesis Assistants

AI-powered research assistants simplify the process of gathering, analyzing, and synthesizing vast amounts of information. These tools assist students, researchers, and professionals in organizing and extracting valuable insights from academic literature and databases.

- AI-Powered Search Engines: Google Scholar, Semantic Scholar, and Elicit use AI to provide relevant and credible academic resources.
- Automated Summarization: AI tools like ChatGPT and Jasper generate concise summaries of complex research papers, making knowledge more accessible.
- Data Analysis and Visualization: AI tools assist in statistical analysis, data modeling, and visualization, crucial for research projects in various fields.

Writing and Creative Development Support

AI plays a significant role in enhancing creative writing and content generation by providing structure, grammar correction, and even idea generation.

- AI Writing Assistants: Grammarly, Hemingway, and Quillbot enhance writing by correcting grammar, improving readability, and suggesting better phrasing.
- Idea Generation Tools: AI-powered brainstorming tools like Sudowrite and Writesonic help generate plot ideas, character development, and story outlines.
- Plagiarism Detection: AI-based plagiarism checkers like Turnitin ensure academic integrity by detecting copied content from online sources.

Language Learning and Translation Services

AI has significantly improved language learning and real-time translation, breaking language barriers and enabling global communication.

- AI-Powered Language Tutors: Apps like Duolingo, Babbel, and Rosetta Stone use AI to personalize lessons and improve language retention.
- Speech Recognition and Pronunciation Feedback: AI tools analyze pronunciation accuracy and provide feedback, helping learners refine their speaking skills.

- Real-Time Translation: AI-based translation tools like Google Translate and DeepL enable seamless multilingual communication across different languages.

Continuous Learning and Skill Development

In the era of rapid technological advancements, continuous learning is essential. AI-driven learning platforms support skill enhancement for professionals and lifelong learners.

- AI-Based Professional Training: Platforms like LinkedIn Learning and Coursera offer AI-recommended courses based on career goals and industry trends.
- AI in Corporate Learning: Companies integrate AI-driven training modules to upskill employees, ensuring workforce adaptability to new technologies.
- Personalized Career Guidance: AI career coaches analyze individual skills and market trends to recommend career paths and professional development opportunities.

Case Study: AI Tutors in K-12 and Higher Education

K-12 Education

AI tutors are transforming primary and secondary education by offering personalized support to students and easing the workload of teachers.

- Example: Squirrel AI: A Chinese EdTech company that uses AI-driven personalized tutoring to help students improve learning efficiency.
- AI-Powered Homework Assistance: Tools like Photomath and Brainly allow students to scan problems and receive step-by-step explanations.

Higher Education

Universities and colleges are integrating AI into their curricula and student support systems.

- Virtual Teaching Assistants: AI assistants like Jill Watson (Georgia Tech) respond to students' queries and streamline administrative tasks.
- Automated Grading and Assessment: AI tools like Gradescope assist educators in grading assignments and providing detailed feedback efficiently.
- AI-Based Research Assistance: Tools like IBM Watson help students conduct research, analyze data, and generate insights in various disciplines.

Conclusion

AI is reshaping the education landscape, offering personalized learning experiences, improving accessibility, and enhancing teaching methodologies. From AI-powered tutors to language learning applications, these innovations foster a more inclusive and effective learning environment.

Chapter 7: Financial Management and Planning

Introduction

Financial management is a crucial aspect of both personal and business success. With the rise of technology, AI-driven tools and automated financial services have revolutionized how individuals and businesses manage their money. This chapter explores the fundamentals of financial management, effective planning strategies, and the role of AI in modern financial decision-making.

Budgeting and Expense Tracking

Understanding Budgeting: Budgeting is the process of planning income and expenses to achieve financial stability. It helps individuals and businesses allocate resources effectively, reduce unnecessary spending, and ensure financial security.

Types of Budgets:

1. Personal Budget: A plan to manage household income and expenses.
2. Business Budget: A strategy to track company revenues, costs, and profitability.
3. Zero-Based Budgeting: Every dollar is assigned a purpose, ensuring no wasted resources.

4. Envelope Budgeting: A cash-based system to allocate specific amounts for different expenses.

Expense Tracking Tools:

- AI-powered apps such as Mint, YNAB, and PocketGuard provide real-time tracking and insights.
- Automated alerts for overspending and category-based spending analysis.
- Integration with banking systems to streamline financial monitoring.

Investment Research and Portfolio Management

The Importance of Investment Planning: Investment is a key factor in wealth creation and financial security. Managing investments effectively requires research, diversification, and risk assessment.

AI in Investment Research:

- Predictive Analytics: AI tools analyze market trends to provide investment recommendations.
- Algorithmic Trading: Automated trading systems execute transactions based on data-driven insights.
- Robo-Advisors: AI-powered financial advisors like Betterment and Wealthfront provide portfolio management based on user risk profiles.

Portfolio Management Strategies:

1. Diversification: Investing in multiple asset classes to reduce risk.
2. Risk Assessment: Evaluating investment risk using AI-powered tools.
3. Passive vs. Active Investing: Choosing between index funds and actively managed portfolios.
4. Rebalancing Strategies: Adjusting portfolio composition to maintain financial goals.

Tax Preparation and Financial Compliance

Understanding Taxation: Taxes are mandatory financial charges imposed by the government. Proper tax planning minimizes liabilities and ensures compliance.

Tax Planning Strategies:

- Income Tax Optimization: Maximizing deductions and tax credits.
- Business Tax Management: Understanding corporate tax structures.
- International Tax Compliance: Managing cross-border taxation regulations.

AI in Tax Preparation:

- Automated Tax Filing: Platforms like TurboTax and H&R Block use AI for quick and accurate tax submissions.

- Error Detection: AI-powered systems identify inconsistencies in tax filings.
- Audit Assistance: AI tools help detect anomalies and prepare responses for tax audits.

Fraud Detection and Security

Financial Fraud Types:

1. Identity Theft: Unauthorized use of personal information.
2. Phishing Scams: Fraudulent attempts to obtain sensitive data.
3. Transaction Fraud: Unauthorized transactions on financial accounts.

AI in Fraud Detection:

- Machine Learning Models: Identify suspicious financial transactions.
- Behavioral Analysis: Detects unusual spending patterns in real time.
- Biometric Security: Enhances authentication using facial recognition and fingerprint scanning.

Best Practices for Financial Security:

- Use multi-factor authentication for banking and investment accounts.
- Regularly monitor credit reports and financial statements.

- Stay updated on the latest cybersecurity threats and financial scams.

Financial Education and Literacy Development

The Importance of Financial Literacy: Financial education empowers individuals to make informed decisions about saving, investing, and managing debt.

Key Areas of Financial Literacy:

1. Savings and Retirement Planning – Understanding 401(k), IRAs, and pension plans.
2. Debt Management – Strategies for handling loans and credit card debt effectively.
3. Understanding Interest Rates – How interest impacts loans and investments.
4. Insurance Planning – Managing risks with life, health, and property insurance.

AI in Financial Education:

- Chatbots and Virtual Advisors: Provide financial guidance through conversational AI.
- Gamified Learning Platforms: Interactive tools to teach financial management skills.
- Personalized Financial Coaching: AI-driven applications analyze spending habits and offer customized tips.

Case Study: AI-Driven Financial Planning for Life Events

Scenario: Emma, a 30-year-old professional, wants to plan for major life events, including buying a home, marriage, and retirement. She uses an AI-powered financial planning tool to create a customized roadmap.

How AI Helps:

- Budget Optimization: AI suggests savings plans based on Emma's income and expenses.
- Investment Guidance: AI recommends diversified investments tailored to her risk profile.
- Retirement Planning: AI simulates different retirement scenarios to optimize contributions.
- Tax Efficiency: The system advises tax-saving strategies based on her financial status.

Outcome: By leveraging AI-driven financial planning, Emma successfully balances short-term expenses and long-term financial goals, securing her financial future.

Conclusion

Financial management and planning are essential for achieving financial stability and growth. With advancements in AI, individuals and businesses can now leverage automated tools for budgeting, investment research, tax compliance, fraud detection, and financial education. By understanding and implementing these strategies, financial success becomes more attainable and efficient.

Chapter 8: Health and Wellness

Health Data Monitoring and Analysis

The advancement of artificial intelligence (AI) in healthcare has revolutionized the way health data is monitored and analyzed. Wearable devices, such as smartwatches and fitness trackers, collect real-time data on heart rate, oxygen levels, sleep patterns, and physical activity. AI algorithms analyze this data to detect anomalies and provide users with actionable insights.

For instance, AI-driven platforms can identify irregular heartbeats or sudden changes in blood pressure, alerting users and medical professionals to potential health risks. Predictive analytics further enhances healthcare by forecasting the likelihood of illnesses such as diabetes or cardiovascular diseases based on historical health data.

Healthcare providers use AI-powered electronic health record (EHR) systems to streamline patient data management. These systems facilitate faster diagnosis and personalized treatment plans, ensuring improved patient care. AI can also integrate genetic information, lifestyle choices, and medical history to recommend preventive measures and treatments tailored to individual patients.

Medication Management and Reminders

One of the most critical aspects of healthcare is proper medication adherence. AI-driven applications and smart pill dispensers help patients take their medications on time, reducing the risks associated with missed doses or overdosing.

These AI tools send reminders via smartphones, smartwatches, or voice assistants, ensuring patients follow their prescribed schedules. Some systems also provide educational content about medications, including potential side effects and drug interactions. For individuals managing multiple medications, AI-powered platforms can create an optimized schedule, minimizing conflicts and enhancing treatment efficacy.

Additionally, AI-driven chatbots assist patients by answering medication-related queries, tracking prescription refills, and notifying caregivers or family members if a dose is missed. This proactive approach significantly benefits elderly patients or individuals with cognitive impairments who require continuous medical assistance.

Fitness Planning and Progress Tracking

AI-powered fitness solutions have transformed how people approach their health and wellness goals. Personalized workout plans, generated through AI analysis, help users achieve their fitness objectives effectively. Whether it's weight loss, muscle gain, or endurance improvement, AI systems analyze body metrics, lifestyle habits, and exercise history to design customized fitness routines.

Wearable devices monitor step counts, calorie burn, and exercise intensity, providing users with real-time feedback. AI algorithms detect patterns in a user's fitness journey and suggest adjustments to optimize performance. Some AI-driven applications also incorporate gamification techniques, encouraging users to stay motivated by rewarding achievements and setting milestones.

Virtual personal trainers, powered by AI, analyze users' form and posture through computer vision technology. These trainers provide instant feedback and corrections, reducing the risk of injury and ensuring workouts are performed correctly. AI integration with augmented reality (AR) also enhances fitness experiences, making exercise more engaging and interactive.

Mental Health Support and Cognitive Behavioral Interventions

AI plays a crucial role in mental health support, offering cognitive behavioral therapy (CBT) interventions, mindfulness exercises, and mood tracking solutions. AI-driven chatbots, such as Woebot and Wysa, provide conversational therapy, helping users manage stress, anxiety, and depression through guided conversations.

These AI mental health assistants analyze user inputs, identify emotional patterns, and offer tailored coping strategies. By leveraging natural language processing (NLP), AI chatbots create a safe and non-judgmental environment where individuals can express their emotions freely.

Mood tracking applications utilize AI to detect emotional fluctuations based on user interactions, social media activity, and speech patterns. AI can also analyze voice tone and facial expressions to assess mental well-being, providing early intervention for individuals at risk of mental health disorders.

Additionally, AI-powered meditation and mindfulness apps help users manage stress through guided breathing exercises, relaxation techniques, and personalized meditation sessions. These tools contribute to overall mental wellness by promoting emotional resilience and mindfulness.

Telemedicine and Healthcare Navigation

Telemedicine has become an essential component of modern healthcare, providing remote consultations, diagnosis, and treatment recommendations through AI-powered platforms. AI-enhanced telemedicine systems allow patients to connect with healthcare professionals via video calls, chatbots, and virtual assistants.

AI-driven diagnostic tools assist doctors in analyzing medical images, lab reports, and patient symptoms. These tools improve diagnostic accuracy, enabling healthcare providers to detect diseases at an early stage. AI-based triage systems assess patients' symptoms and recommend appropriate healthcare actions, reducing the burden on hospitals and emergency rooms.

Healthcare navigation platforms utilize AI to help patients find suitable healthcare providers, schedule appointments, and access relevant medical resources. AI-powered virtual nurses offer guidance on managing common illnesses, post-operative care, and chronic disease management, empowering patients to make informed healthcare decisions.

Case Study: Managing Chronic Conditions with AI Support

Background

John, a 55-year-old man diagnosed with type 2 diabetes and hypertension, struggled with managing his chronic conditions. His irregular medication intake, lack of exercise, and unmonitored glucose levels led to frequent health complications.

AI-Driven Solution

John's healthcare provider introduced an AI-powered health management system to help him track his health metrics, maintain his medication schedule, and adopt a healthier lifestyle.

1. AI-Powered Health Monitoring: John wore a smartwatch that continuously tracked his glucose

levels, heart rate, and physical activity. AI analyzed these readings and alerted him and his doctor if any irregularities were detected.

2. Medication Reminders: A smart medication dispenser ensured he took his pills on time. AI-generated alerts reminded him of his dosage schedule and sent notifications to his caregiver if he missed a dose.

3. Fitness and Diet Recommendations: Based on John's health data, an AI fitness coach recommended personalized exercise routines. Additionally, an AI-driven nutrition assistant suggested meal plans optimized for his dietary needs.

4. Mental Health Support: Since managing chronic illnesses can be stressful, John used an AI-powered mental health chatbot that provided cognitive behavioral interventions, relaxation exercises, and stress management techniques.

5. Telemedicine Support: John had virtual consultations with his doctor through an AI-powered telemedicine platform, ensuring consistent medical supervision without frequent hospital visits.

Outcome

With the AI-driven health management system, John experienced significant improvements in his overall well-being. His blood sugar levels stabilized, his adherence to medication improved, and his stress levels decreased. The AI intervention enhanced his quality of life, demonstrating the potential of AI in managing chronic conditions effectively.

This chapter highlights the transformative impact of AI in health and wellness. From real-time health monitoring to AI-driven mental health support, these advancements pave the way for a healthier and more efficient healthcare ecosystem. As AI technology continues to evolve, its role in healthcare will only expand, offering smarter solutions for personalized and preventive medicine.

Chapter 9: Large Language Models and Foundation Models

Introduction

Large Language Models (LLMs) and foundation models have transformed artificial intelligence by enabling machines to understand and generate human-like text, code, and even images. These models serve as the backbone for various AI applications, including chatbots, content creation, search engines, and virtual assistants. In this chapter, we explore their architecture, training methodologies, fine-tuning techniques, optimization strategies, and future advancements.

The Architecture of Modern LLMs

LLMs rely on deep neural networks built on the Transformer architecture, introduced by Vaswani et al. in 2017. Key components include:

1. Transformer-Based Structure

- Self-Attention Mechanism: Allows the model to weigh the importance of different words in a sentence, enabling context-awareness.
- Multi-Head Attention: Enhances the model's ability to capture diverse linguistic patterns.

- Positional Encoding: Provides sequential order information to the model, overcoming the limitations of traditional RNNs and LSTMs.

2. Model Scaling

- Larger models, such as GPT-4 and Claude, utilize billions of parameters to improve accuracy and fluency.
- Scaling laws indicate that larger datasets and model sizes lead to better generalization.

3. Memory and Computation Challenges

- High computational costs require specialized hardware like TPUs (Tensor Processing Units) and GPUs.
- Efficient memory management is crucial for handling large-scale models.

Training Methodologies and Data Requirements

LLMs are trained using vast amounts of data and computational resources. Key training methodologies include:

1. Pretraining on Large Datasets

- Models learn from diverse sources such as books, scientific papers, news articles, and web data.
- Pretraining involves unsupervised learning, where models predict missing words in sentences (Masked Language Modeling in BERT) or predict the next word in a sequence (Autoregressive Modeling in GPT).

2. Reinforcement Learning from Human Feedback (RLHF)

- Used to align AI models with human values and preferences.
- Incorporates reward models that rank outputs based on human feedback.

3. Continual Learning and Adaptation

- Techniques like transfer learning allow models to adapt to new domains with minimal retraining.
- Ongoing updates help LLMs stay relevant with evolving information.

Fine-Tuning and Specialization Techniques

Once pretrained, models undergo fine-tuning to specialize in specific domains, improving their performance.

1. Domain-Specific Fine-Tuning

- Medical AI models trained on healthcare datasets (e.g., BioGPT).
- Legal AI models fine-tuned on case law and legal documents.

2. Prompt Engineering

- Crafting effective prompts enhances model responses without modifying parameters.
- Techniques like zero-shot, few-shot, and chain-of-thought prompting improve reasoning.

3. Parameter-Efficient Fine-Tuning (PEFT)

- Techniques like LoRA (Low-Rank Adaptation) and Adapters reduce computational costs while fine-tuning.

Inference Optimization and Deployment Strategies

Deploying LLMs requires balancing performance and efficiency. Key strategies include:

1. Model Quantization

- Reduces model size by lowering numerical precision (e.g., converting 32-bit to 8-bit).
- Speeds up inference with minimal loss of accuracy.

2. Distillation Techniques

- Knowledge Distillation creates smaller, faster models while retaining knowledge from larger models.
- Student models mimic teacher models with reduced parameters.

3. Edge and Cloud Deployment

- Edge AI enables models to run on local devices (smartphones, IoT devices).
- Cloud-based APIs (e.g., OpenAI's API, Google's PaLM) provide scalable access to LLMs.

The Evolution from Models to Multimodal Systems

Traditional LLMs process only text, but multimodal AI models integrate various data types:

1. Vision-Language Models

- Examples: GPT-4V, DALL·E, and CLIP

- These models understand and generate both text and images.

2. Speech-Language Models

- Examples: Whisper, Meta's SeamlessM4T
- Enable voice assistants, transcription services, and real-time translation.

3. Video and 3D Model Integration

- Future AI models will process videos and 3D spatial data, revolutionizing industries like gaming, virtual reality, and digital marketing.

Limitations and Challenges in LLM Development

Despite their advancements, LLMs face several challenges:

1. Ethical and Bias Issues

- LLMs may reflect biases present in training data, leading to discriminatory outputs.
- Continuous efforts in bias mitigation and fairness evaluation are necessary.

2. High Computational Costs

- Training and deploying large models require immense energy and resources.
- Research on energy-efficient AI is gaining traction.

3. Hallucination Problems

- LLMs sometimes generate factually incorrect or misleading information.
- Fact-checking and retrieval-augmented generation (RAG) techniques help address this issue.

4. Security Risks

- Prompt injection attacks can manipulate model behavior.
- Safeguarding AI models against adversarial exploits is crucial.

Conclusion

Large Language Models and foundation models are shaping the future of AI-powered applications. While they bring remarkable advancements in automation, creativity, and problem-solving, they also introduce challenges that researchers and developers must address. The evolution from text-based models to multimodal AI marks the next frontier in artificial intelligence, unlocking new possibilities for industries worldwide.

Chapter 10: Reasoning and Decision-Making Capabilities

Introduction

Traditional artificial intelligence models excel at pattern matching, but true intelligence requires reasoning, decision-making, and planning. Modern AI systems, including Large Language Models (LLMs), have made strides in reasoning through structured approaches such as Chain-of-Thought (CoT) and Tree-of-Thought (ToT) techniques. Additionally, AI's ability to integrate external tools, plan sequential actions, and collaborate with other agents is driving innovation in real-world applications. However, AI reasoning still faces challenges in accuracy, consistency, and adaptability.

This chapter explores AI's journey from simple pattern recognition to complex reasoning and decision-making capabilities, highlighting current methodologies, real-world applications, and limitations.

From Pattern Matching to Reasoning

Early AI systems relied on rule-based pattern matching rather than genuine reasoning. These systems could:

- Identify predefined patterns in data.

- Apply heuristics to solve specific tasks (e.g., expert systems in medical diagnosis).
- Use probabilistic models to estimate outcomes.

However, these approaches lacked generalizable reasoning skills. Modern AI, powered by deep learning and LLMs, has shifted towards contextual understanding, logical deduction, and multi-step problem-solving.

Key Milestones in AI Reasoning Evolution

1. Symbolic AI (1960s-1980s) – Based on logic and knowledge representation (e.g., expert systems).
2. Machine Learning (1990s-2010s) – Shift from rules to statistical learning.
3. Neural Networks & Transformers (2017-Present) – Deep learning models capable of complex reasoning tasks.
4. Emergent Reasoning Techniques – Advances like Chain-of-Thought prompting enhance multi-step reasoning.

Chain-of-Thought and Tree-of-Thought Approaches

Modern AI reasoning techniques focus on breaking down problems into logical steps rather than providing instant answers.

1. Chain-of-Thought (CoT) Reasoning

- A prompting technique where models generate step-by-step solutions rather than immediate answers.
- Helps in complex math, logic, and decision-making tasks.
- Example:
  Prompt: "If John has 3 apples and buys 5 more, how many does he have?"
  CoT Output: "John starts with 3 apples. He buys 5 more. 3 + 5 = 8. Answer: 8 apples."

2. Tree-of-Thought (ToT) Reasoning

- Extends CoT by exploring multiple reasoning paths simultaneously.
- Useful for strategic decision-making (e.g., chess, robotics).
- Example: AI considers different possible answers and ranks them based on probabilities.

Key Difference:

Approach	Explanation	Use Case Example
CoT	Single logical path	Math problems, logical reasoning

ToT	Multiple branching paths	Game playing, strategic planning

Planning and Sequential Decision Making

AI systems that interact with dynamic environments must plan and make sequential decisions.

1. Reinforcement Learning (RL) for Decision Making

- AI learns through trial and error, optimizing for rewards.
- Example: AlphaGo mastering Go through self-play.

2. Hierarchical Planning in AI

- AI models break down goals into smaller tasks.
- Example: A robotic assistant planning a sequence of actions to complete a household chore.

3. Real-World Applications of AI Planning

- Autonomous Vehicles: AI predicts road conditions and adjusts driving decisions.

- Healthcare AI: AI suggests treatment plans based on patient history.
- Financial Forecasting: AI models predict stock trends based on historical data.

Tool Use and External System Integration

Modern AI systems are not limited to internal knowledge—they integrate with external tools and databases for enhanced reasoning.

1. API and Plugin Integration

- AI models can interact with search engines, databases, and APIs for real-time information.
- Example: ChatGPT using Wolfram Alpha for mathematical computations.

2. Code Execution and Automated Problem Solving

- AI-powered coding assistants like GitHub Copilot generate and test code.
- Example: AI writing SQL queries to fetch database records.

3. AI-Assisted Research and Analysis

- AI can process scientific papers and summarize key insights.
- Example: AI analyzing clinical trial data to identify new drug treatments.

Multi-Agent Systems and Collaborative Problem Solving

Instead of a single AI making decisions, multi-agent systems collaborate to solve complex problems.

1. What Are Multi-Agent Systems?

- Multiple AI models or bots work together, each specializing in different tasks.
- Inspired by human teamwork and swarm intelligence.

2. Applications of Multi-Agent AI

- Supply Chain Management: AI agents optimize logistics across multiple warehouses.
- Financial Trading: AI agents analyze and execute trades based on real-time data.
- Gaming & Simulations: AI NPCs in video games coordinate actions dynamically.

3. Challenges in Multi-Agent Collaboration

- Coordination Complexity: Ensuring all agents work together efficiently.
- Conflict Resolution: Handling disagreements between AI agents.
- Scalability Issues: Managing thousands of agents simultaneously.

Current Limitations in AI Reasoning

Despite rapid advancements, AI reasoning still faces several challenges:

1. Lack of True Understanding

- AI models generate plausible responses without true comprehension.
- Example: AI providing incorrect yet confident-sounding answers.

2. Contextual Errors & Logical Fallacies

- AI struggles with long-term memory and context retention.
- Example: Losing track of facts in multi-turn conversations.

3. Over-Reliance on Training Data

- AI reasoning is limited to what it has seen before.

- Challenge: How to make AI generalize reasoning beyond training data.

4. Ethical and Decision-Making Risks

- AI may exhibit biases in decision-making.
- Example: Biased hiring algorithms rejecting certain candidates.

5. Real-World Uncertainty Handling

- AI struggles with unpredictable real-world variables (e.g., weather, human behavior).
- Ongoing research in probabilistic AI aims to address this.

Conclusion

AI's ability to reason and make decisions has evolved significantly, from basic pattern matching to advanced multi-step reasoning, planning, and collaboration. Techniques like Chain-of-Thought and Tree-of-Thought reasoning have improved AI's problem-solving skills, while multi-agent systems enable teamwork across AI models. However, AI reasoning still has fundamental limitations, requiring further advancements in logic, ethics, and adaptability.

As AI research progresses, the goal is to create AI systems that can reason as effectively as humans, making reliable, unbiased, and ethical decisions in complex environments.

Chapter 11: AI Agent Deployment Technologies

Introduction

The deployment of AI agents is a critical phase in artificial intelligence applications, ensuring that models operate efficiently, securely, and in real-world scenarios. AI agents—whether virtual assistants, chatbots, autonomous systems, or recommendation engines—must be optimized for performance, scalability, and adaptability.

This chapter explores the various deployment architectures, from cloud-based and on-device solutions to edge computing, security frameworks, multimodal input processing, and system integration strategies.

Cloud-Based vs. On-Device Processing

AI agents can be deployed using two primary approaches: cloud-based processing and on-device (local) processing. Each has its own advantages and trade-offs, depending on application requirements.

1. Cloud-Based AI Processing

Cloud computing allows AI models to run on remote servers, offering high scalability, computational power, and seamless updates.

Advantages:

- High Processing Power: Cloud servers utilize powerful GPUs and TPUs for AI workloads.
- Continuous Model Updates: AI models can be frequently updated without requiring user intervention.
- Cross-Device Synchronization: Enables AI agents to function across multiple devices seamlessly.

Challenges:

- Latency Issues: Network dependency may introduce delays.
- Privacy Concerns: Sensitive data transmitted to cloud servers poses security risks.
- Ongoing Costs: Requires cloud infrastructure expenses.

2. On-Device AI Processing

On-device AI processing runs models locally on smartphones, IoT devices, or embedded systems, reducing reliance on external servers.

Advantages:

- Low Latency: Real-time responses without internet dependency.
- Enhanced Privacy: Data remains on the device, reducing security risks.
- Lower Operational Costs: No recurring cloud server fees.

Challenges:

- Limited Processing Power: Devices have lower computational capabilities than cloud servers.
- Storage Constraints: AI models may need compression techniques like quantization.

Edge Computing for AI Agents

Edge computing bridges the gap between cloud and on-device processing by handling computations closer to the data source (e.g., IoT devices, autonomous vehicles).

Key Benefits of Edge AI:

1. Reduced Latency – AI processing occurs at the network edge, minimizing delays.
2. Bandwidth Optimization – Decreases cloud data transmission, saving costs.
3. Offline Functionality – AI agents remain operational even without an internet connection.
4. Energy Efficiency – Reduces power consumption by distributing AI tasks efficiently.

Use Cases of Edge AI:

- Autonomous Vehicles: Real-time decision-making without cloud reliance.
- Smart Surveillance Systems: AI-powered security cameras analyze threats locally.
- Wearable AI Devices: Smartwatches process health data on the device.

Edge AI is crucial for applications requiring real-time responses, privacy preservation, and energy-efficient computing.

Data Privacy and Security Architectures

AI agent deployments must prioritize data security and user privacy to prevent breaches, unauthorized access, and compliance violations.

1. Secure Data Transmission

- End-to-End Encryption: Protects data from interception.
- Federated Learning: AI training occurs on local devices, reducing data transfer risks.

2. Differential Privacy

- Adds mathematical noise to AI models, preventing data leakage.

3. AI Governance & Compliance

- Adheres to regulations like GDPR, CCPA, and HIPAA to protect user data.

4. Threat Detection Mechanisms

- AI Model Watermarking: Prevents unauthorized usage.
- Adversarial Robustness: Detects malicious AI manipulations.

Security-first deployment ensures AI agents remain ethical, transparent, and trustworthy.

Multimodal Input Processing Pipelines

Modern AI agents process multiple input types—text, speech, images, and video—to provide richer interactions. This is known as multimodal AI.

Components of Multimodal AI Processing:

1. Text Processing: NLP models analyze language input.
2. Speech Recognition: Converts voice commands into text (e.g., Whisper AI).
3. Computer Vision: Extracts information from images and videos.
4. Sensor Integration: AI agents interpret data from IoT sensors.

Example Applications:

- Smart Assistants (Alexa, Siri, Google Assistant) – Understands text, voice, and images.
- Healthcare AI – Processes medical scans alongside patient history.
- Retail AI – Analyzes shopping behavior via speech and video analytics.

Seamless fusion of multimodal inputs enables AI agents to operate in complex, real-world scenarios.

Context Maintenance and Memory Systems

AI agents need context awareness to provide human-like interactions, remembering previous conversations and learning from user behavior.

Types of AI Memory Systems:

1. Short-Term Memory (Session-Based)

- Maintains user context for a single interaction.
- Used in chatbots and voice assistants.

2. Long-Term Memory (Persistent AI Memory)

- Stores user preferences over time.
- Used in personalized recommendations (e.g., Netflix, Spotify).

3. Knowledge Graphs & Vector Databases

- Helps AI agents retrieve and connect past information.
- Examples: OpenAI's Retrieval-Augmented Generation (RAG), Google's Knowledge Graph.

Challenges in Context Maintenance:

- Memory Overload: Managing vast user interactions efficiently.
- Privacy Trade-Offs: Storing user history while respecting data security.

Context-aware AI enhances engagement by personalizing responses based on previous interactions.

System Integration and API Ecosystems

For AI agents to function in real-world applications, they must integrate seamlessly with various platforms and services via APIs (Application Programming Interfaces).

1. API-Driven AI Deployment

- RESTful APIs: Common for web-based AI services.
- GraphQL APIs: Efficient for querying structured AI data.
- WebSockets: Enables real-time communication (e.g., AI-powered chatbots).

2. Cloud-Based AI API Providers

Provider	AI Services
OpenAI	ChatGPT, DALL·E, Whisper
Google Cloud AI	Vertex AI, Speech-to-Text
Amazon AWS AI	Lex, Rekognition, SageMaker
Microsoft Azure AI	Cognitive Services, Chatbot APIs

3. Enterprise AI Integration

- ERP & CRM Systems: AI agents automate business workflows.
- IoT & Smart Devices: AI agents control home automation systems.

APIs allow scalable, modular AI deployment across industries.

Conclusion

Deploying AI agents requires choosing the right balance between cloud, edge, and on-device processing while ensuring security, multimodal capabilities, and seamless system integration. With advancements in privacy-preserving AI, context-aware memory, and multimodal input handling, AI agents are becoming more adaptive, responsive, and intelligent.

The next frontier in AI deployment lies in real-time, decentralized, and privacy-enhanced AI agents, powering the future of automation, personalization, and human-AI collaboration.

Chapter 12: Ethical Considerations and Challenges

Introduction

Artificial Intelligence (AI) is rapidly transforming society, influencing industries, economies, and personal lives. While its capabilities continue to expand, so do the ethical dilemmas surrounding its use. The widespread adoption of AI raises critical concerns about privacy, transparency, dependency, accessibility, regulations, and ethical design. In this chapter, we explore these challenges and discuss how AI can be developed and implemented responsibly to ensure fairness, accountability, and societal well-being.

Privacy Concerns in the Age of Omnipresent AI

With AI embedded in smartphones, surveillance systems, social media, and healthcare, the erosion of privacy is a growing issue.

1. Data Collection and Surveillance

- AI systems collect vast amounts of personal data through web tracking, smart assistants, and biometric recognition.

- Governments and corporations leverage AI for mass surveillance, raising concerns about civil liberties.
- Unchecked data collection can lead to intrusive profiling, discrimination, and privacy breaches.

2. Data Ownership and Consent

- Many users are unaware of how their data is used, stored, or shared.
- Lack of explicit consent mechanisms leads to unethical data exploitation.
- The right to be forgotten and user-controlled data ownership are emerging debates.

3. AI in Cybersecurity and Data Breaches

- AI can enhance cybersecurity but also be weaponized for hacking and identity theft.
- AI-driven phishing and deepfake scams are on the rise, challenging traditional security measures.
- Protecting sensitive personal data is crucial for maintaining public trust in AI systems.

Transparency and Explainability of AI Agent Decisions

Many AI models operate as black boxes, making it difficult to understand their decision-making process.

1. Black-Box Problem in AI

- Complex deep-learning models, such as neural networks and transformers, lack interpretability.
- AI-powered financial lending, medical diagnoses, and legal judgments need to be explainable to ensure fairness.

2. Importance of Explainable AI (XAI)

- Explainable AI (XAI) focuses on making AI decisions understandable for users.
- XAI techniques include attention mechanisms, decision trees, and rule-based systems.
- Regulatory bodies demand algorithmic accountability for high-risk AI applications.

3. Trust and Public Acceptance

- Lack of transparency can lead to distrust in AI systems.
- AI-driven misinformation and biased outcomes can damage credibility.
- Ethical AI must prioritize clarity, auditability, and user interpretability.

Dependency and Autonomy: Finding the Right Balance

AI is increasingly automating decision-making processes, but overreliance on AI poses risks.

1. Overdependence on AI Systems

- Autonomous vehicles, medical AI, and AI-driven financial trading reduce human intervention.
- If systems fail, human decision-makers may lack the skills to intervene effectively.
- AI should act as an assistive tool rather than fully replacing human judgment.

2. The Autonomy vs. Human Oversight Debate

- Fully autonomous AI risks unintended consequences.
- Human-in-the-loop (HITL) approaches integrate human oversight into AI decision-making.
- Hybrid AI-Human collaboration ensures better ethical and practical outcomes.

3. Ethical Risks of AI Replacing Human Roles

- AI-driven automation may displace workers across industries.
- Ethical considerations must include job reskilling programs and fair labor transitions.

Digital Divides and Accessibility Challenges

The benefits of AI should be accessible to all, yet disparities in AI availability widen existing social and economic inequalities.

1. Global AI Inequality

- Wealthier nations have better AI infrastructure, while developing regions lack resources.
- AI-driven automation benefits tech-driven economies, but low-income workers face job displacement.
- Bridging the AI knowledge gap is crucial for equitable technological progress.

2. Accessibility for Marginalized Communities

- AI tools must be designed for disabled users (e.g., voice-based interfaces, adaptive AI).
- Biased datasets often exclude or misrepresent certain populations.
- AI training datasets should be diverse, representative, and bias-free.

3. Algorithmic Bias and Fairness

- AI systems may unintentionally reinforce gender, racial, or cultural biases.
- Case studies show biased AI in hiring algorithms, facial recognition, and criminal justice.
- Developers must implement bias-detection mechanisms and fair AI modeling techniques.

Regulatory Frameworks and Industry Standards

AI regulations are evolving to address risks and ensure responsible AI development.

1. AI Governance and Legal Frameworks

- The EU's AI Act categorizes AI applications based on risk levels.
- The US AI Bill of Rights proposes transparency, fairness, and privacy safeguards.
- China, India, and Japan are also developing AI regulatory policies.

2. Ethical AI Certification and Compliance

- Tech companies are implementing AI ethics boards and independent audits.
- AI models must comply with GDPR (General Data Protection Regulation) and CCPA (California Consumer Privacy Act) for data protection.

3. Balancing Innovation and Regulation

- Over-regulation can stifle AI innovation, while under-regulation may lead to harmful AI deployments.
- Governments, industry leaders, and researchers must collaborate on ethical AI policies.

Building Ethical Considerations into AI Development

Developers and AI researchers must embed ethics into AI systems from the ground up.

1. Ethical AI Design Principles

- Fairness: AI should be unbiased and inclusive.
- Accountability: Developers should be responsible for AI outcomes.
- Transparency: Users should understand how AI decisions are made.
- Privacy-first approach: AI should minimize unnecessary data collection.

2. Human-Centric AI Development

- AI should enhance human decision-making, not replace it.
- User feedback loops should refine AI models.
- Ethical AI should prioritize safety, inclusivity, and fairness.

3. Future Challenges in Ethical AI

- As AI becomes more autonomous, ethical considerations must evolve.
- AI consciousness and rights debates may emerge with advanced AGI models.
- Ethical frameworks must adapt to AI's rapid advancements.

Conclusion

The ethical challenges surrounding AI are complex but addressable with responsible development, governance, and regulation. Privacy, fairness, transparency, and accessibility must be prioritized to ensure AI benefits everyone rather than a select few. The future of AI depends on the collective efforts of policymakers, developers, businesses, and users to create systems that are both powerful and ethical.

By embedding human values into AI design, we can build a future where AI serves society responsibly and equitably.

Chapter 13: The Future of AI Agents

Introduction

AI agents are rapidly evolving, moving beyond simple automation towards intelligent, self-learning, and highly autonomous systems. As advancements in deep learning, reinforcement learning, and multimodal AI unfold, we are witnessing a shift toward more specialized and general-purpose AI agents capable of reasoning, adapting, and even interacting with the physical world.

This chapter explores the cutting-edge research shaping AI agents, the balance between specialized and general-purpose AI, the future of autonomous systems, the integration of AI with robotics, and the evolving human-AI relationship. We also project a timeline (2025–2035) for upcoming breakthroughs in AI agent technology.

Emerging Research Directions and Coming Breakthroughs

The next decade will bring transformative breakthroughs in AI agents. Key areas of research include:

1. Self-Improving AI Agents

- Future AI agents will continuously improve themselves through self-learning algorithms, reducing the need for human intervention.
- Recursive self-improvement (RSI) techniques will enable AI agents to update their knowledge dynamically.

2. Advanced Reasoning and Decision-Making

- AI agents will transition from statistical pattern recognition to logical reasoning, allowing them to solve complex problems independently.
- Research into neural symbolic AI (combining neural networks with symbolic logic) will enhance decision-making abilities.

3. Multi-Agent Collaboration

- AI agents will be able to coordinate and collaborate, forming networks of autonomous systems that work together on tasks.
- Decentralized AI models will eliminate reliance on central servers, leading to more scalable and privacy-focused solutions.

4. Personalized AI and Emotional Intelligence

- AI agents will develop emotional intelligence to better understand human emotions and context.
- Adaptive personality models will enable AI to align with human preferences, making interactions more natural and engaging.

Specialized vs. General-Purpose Agents

One of the major debates in AI development is whether the future belongs to specialized or general-purpose AI agents.

Specialized AI Agents

- Designed for specific tasks, such as AI-powered doctors, legal assistants, or financial advisors.
- Optimized for performance in a narrow field, leading to greater accuracy and efficiency.
- Examples: AlphaFold (protein folding AI), Codex (AI coding assistant), and Waymo (self-driving AI).

General-Purpose AI Agents

- Capable of handling multiple tasks across various domains.
- Designed with broad intelligence to adapt, learn, and apply knowledge across different fields.
- Examples: GPT-4, Gemini, and Claude—these models can answer questions, generate creative content, and assist in coding, all within the same system.

The Future Outlook: Hybrid AI Agents

- AI development may shift towards hybrid models that combine specialized intelligence with general adaptability.
- AI agents could have modular intelligence, where they integrate specialized skills on demand, making them both efficient and versatile.

The Path to More Autonomous Systems

The goal of AI research is to create truly autonomous systems that require minimal human supervision. Some key developments on this path include:

1. Autonomous Decision-Making

- AI agents will assess risks, set goals, and execute actions without human intervention.
- Reinforcement learning advancements will help AI agents navigate unpredictable environments.

2. Self-Healing AI Systems

- Future AI agents will be able to identify and fix errors in real time without external input.
- AI-powered cybersecurity will allow AI agents to protect themselves from cyber threats.

3. Goal-Driven AI

- AI agents will define their own goals based on long-term objectives rather than executing predefined instructions.
- Autonomous research AI could lead to self-generated scientific discoveries and innovations.

Integration of Robotics and Physical World Capabilities

AI agents will move beyond software and integrate with robotics and physical environments. Some advancements in this area include:

1. AI-Powered Robotics

- Robots will understand natural language and execute commands with improved precision.
- AI agents will control drones, self-driving cars, and industrial robots with real-world intelligence.

2. Digital Twins and AI Simulations

- AI will be used to create virtual replicas of physical environments for training and decision-making.
- NASA, Tesla, and medical research institutions are already using AI-driven simulations to predict real-world outcomes.

3. AI-Powered Smart Infrastructure

- AI agents will be embedded into smart cities, automated supply chains, and energy grids to optimize real-world systems.
- Intelligent disaster response AI will predict and mitigate the impact of natural disasters.

The Evolution of Human-AI Relationships

As AI agents become more advanced, their role in human society will continue to evolve. Key trends include:

1. AI as Personal Assistants

- AI companions will offer hyper-personalized assistance, improving productivity and well-being.
- AI-driven coaching and therapy bots will provide emotional and psychological support.

2. Human-AI Collaboration in Workplaces

- AI will automate repetitive tasks, allowing humans to focus on creativity and strategic thinking.
- The rise of co-pilot AI systems (like Microsoft Copilot and ChatGPT Pro) will redefine professional workflows.

3. Ethical and Societal Challenges

- Ethical concerns around AI consciousness, decision-making power, and data privacy will become more pressing.
- Governments and policymakers will introduce AI governance frameworks to regulate AI agent development and deployment.

Timeline of Expected Developments (2025–2035)

Here is a projected timeline for major advancements in AI agent technology:

2025–2027: AI Becomes More Adaptive and Specialized

- AI assistants become more personalized and context-aware.
- AI-powered robotics enter industries like construction and agriculture.
- Ethical AI frameworks are introduced for fair and responsible AI governance.

2028–2030: AI Autonomy and Real-World Integration

- AI agents will achieve near-human reasoning capabilities.

- Fully autonomous vehicles and AI-driven research labs will emerge.
- AI-human collaboration expands into art, science, and policy-making.

2031–2035: General-Purpose AI and AI-Supervised Societies

- AI agents will manage large-scale systems, such as entire cities, healthcare networks, and financial markets.
- AI will advance towards Artificial General Intelligence (AGI), capable of human-level reasoning.
- Neural-Interface AI (brain-computer interfaces) may enable direct communication between humans and AI.

Conclusion

The future of AI agents is poised for exponential growth, from advanced reasoning and autonomy to deep integration with robotics and human society. Whether specialized or general-purpose, AI agents will play a pivotal role in reshaping industries, economies, and even human relationships.

As we move toward autonomous AI systems, ethical considerations, safety measures, and governance structures will be crucial in ensuring a future where AI serves as a collaborative force rather than a disruptive one.

The next decade will be a defining era for AI agency, autonomy, and its profound impact on our world.

FINAL CONCLUSION

Embracing the AI-Assisted Future

The future of AI agents is no longer a distant vision—it is unfolding right before our eyes. From specialized assistants that enhance productivity to autonomous systems capable of making independent decisions, AI is revolutionizing the way we work, live, and interact with technology. These advancements promise a future where AI seamlessly integrates into every aspect of human life, augmenting human capabilities rather than replacing them.

However, as we embrace this AI-driven transformation, we must remain conscious of the challenges that come with it. Ethical considerations, data privacy, security risks, and the potential displacement of human labor must be addressed proactively. Responsible AI development and transparent regulatory frameworks will play a critical role in ensuring that AI remains a force for good.

Maintaining Human Agency in an Automated World

While AI agents are becoming increasingly autonomous, it is crucial to maintain human control and agency over their development and deployment. AI should serve as an enabler, enhancing human decision-making rather than dictating it.

To achieve this balance, the following principles must be upheld:

1. Human-Centric AI Design – AI should be developed with clear ethical guidelines that prioritize human well-being and empowerment.
2. Transparency and Accountability – AI systems should be explainable, allowing users to understand how decisions are made.
3. Collaboration Over Replacement – AI should complement human skills rather than compete with them, fostering a symbiotic relationship.
4. Lifelong Learning and Adaptation – Humans must continuously learn and adapt alongside AI to remain relevant in an evolving technological landscape.

By ensuring ethical and responsible AI development, we can create a future where AI serves as a partner in progress rather than an uncontrollable force.

Final Thoughts on Human-AI Collaboration

The next decade will redefine the boundaries between human intelligence and artificial intelligence. AI agents will become more adaptive, capable, and intuitive, shaping a future where humans and AI work together in harmony.

Rather than fearing AI, we should embrace it as a powerful tool that enhances creativity, productivity, and problem-solving abilities. The key to a successful AI-driven future lies not in resisting automation but in leveraging AI to create new opportunities, industries, and ways of thinking.

As we stand on the brink of an AI revolution, we must remember: the future of AI is not just about technology—it's about the choices we make today. The responsibility lies with us to guide AI development in a direction that benefits all of humanity.

Copyrights

www.ingramcontent.com/pod-product-compliance
Lightning Source LLC
LaVergne TN
LVHW051656050326
832903LV00032B/3856